LAGAHOO POEMS

Also by James Christopher Aboud, *The Stone Rose*

LAGAHOO POEMS

JAMES CHRISTOPHER ABOUD

PEEPAL TREE

First published in Great Britain in 2004
Reprinted 2007, 2011
Peepal Tree Press Ltd
17 King's Avenue
Leeds LS6 1QS

ISBN 9781900715843

Supported by
ARTS COUNCIL
ENGLAND

for Emily, Rebecca
and Vivien, and in memory
of Ewart Thorne, Q.C.

CONTENTS

I remember him from childhood. I was running home, up Hermitage Road in Belmont. It was already getting dark.

Tall, dressed in a black suit, he smelt like mothballs. I vividly remember his eyes, bulging red, staring as if he knew me. That night, I could still feel his eyes on me. Tantie Rosa said he was probably on his way to Lapeyrouse Cemetery to dig up grave dirt with a black penny.

She told me other things. Lagahoo could change his shape into any beast or form and roam the streets or forests. In order to see him properly, you had to put the *yampee* or mucus from a dog's eye in your own eye and look through your keyhole at midnight. Sometimes, people saw him with a coffin on his head and chains dragging behind. He lusted after girls and women without restraint. In everyday life, he could be an Obeah man, or even a man of some learning, living a quiet, solitary life. He was a genius at maiming or killing. People said that sometimes he became so tall that his head disappeared above the trees. Everyone feared and hid from him.

Grandma told me to say my prayers that night. I did. Twice.

Gerard Besson, *Folklore of Trinidad and Tobago*

The Accused was charged with causing grievous bodily harm to a fellow villager. He had chopped the man with a machete. His defence was that the victim was a Lagahoo who had taken the shape of a beast and was spying on his daughter. In order to succeed, the Accused had to satisfy the jury that he genuinely believed that the victim was a Lagahoo. The Prosecutor described this as a sham defence based on superstition. The Prosecution's first witness was the old man who discovered the bleeding victim. He told the Court that he found the victim on the side of the road near to the home of the accused. He reported that the victim said these words: "Look how Ram chop me". The Prosecutor took his seat with satisfaction and the Judge invited the Defence Attorney to cross-examine the witness.

"You ever see a Lagahoo?" The Defence Attorney boldly asked.

"No", he replied with assurance. Then, after a short pause, during which the whole defence team held its breath, he added, "but I does hear dem bawling in the night".

An account of a criminal trial in Trinidad in 1988
as reported by a member of the defence team.

THE BEGINNING

I will take you to the source
Of the terrible past:
Sun begat moon   Moon begat ocean
Ocean twisted its configuration
Into paper which begat
Countless stories splashed on sand.

Out of sand, the graven image.
The moon shone on it.
The wind whipped past its ankles.
Twenty-eight miles tall,
It grew and grew.

Shadows fell from it,
Making night into more night.
Out of the darkness flew Papa Bois
And he dipped his finger
Into the Atlantic ocean
And so begat whirlwinds,
Staircases of water that twisted skywards –
And some of it fell into the wells
That pierced the flatlands
And out of them came the creatures
Whose hearts pumped eternal night,
And their shapes were diabolic.

Through towns and villages
The great shadow crossed
And rain followed it
Swept along the current of its black cloak,
Flinging itself hard as channa to the Earth,
And splintering.

That was when Lagahoo awoke
And rubbed his eyes, muttering
"This crap must stop".

And he crawled thirteen miles
To the foot of the monstrous image
And on its toe
Wrote his name with an oar.

So it was that earth devoured sand
And light, the darkness,
And Lagahoo, unimpressed,
Built a great bonfire
And combed his hair
While Papa Bois and his children wept.

Fire begat heat
And heat, the frenzy of dancers
Free at last to dance at night,
And Lagahoo said to them:

> *This fire and this heat*
> *will never be divided.*

And evening came
And moonbeams begat lovers
And lovers spoke in whispers,
Soothing the island to sleep.

LAGAHOO DISCOVERS GRAVITY

You see this world,
this world can collapse like a cavern,
                              from inside.

I spring from branches but branches
do not catch me.

The earth is soft and is always
sucking things down.

It is through strength
that I am not sucked in.

When the men sleep
they lie flat to the dirt
and much noise of complaining they make
on rising,
as if climbing trees.

Much is sucked in:
Sky, water, old trees and bodies.
All their life the men fight;
their cheeks hang downwards after awhile;
so too their women's breasts start swinging.
A time comes when their bodies weaken
and the earth forever claims them.

By the hundred teeth of my jaws
I'll not submit.

The earth will have to carry too the hills
and the big boulders
before I am drowned in it.

MORE COLOURED ANIMALS

Stay awhile Christopher Columbus,
the flags above your boats
look pretty in the wind.

Still they dance
Still they dance
as evening darkens hill
and your sharp metals.

Stay awhile Christopher Columbus,
your skin is blue
your lips are pink –
a happier animal than you
in any jungle
I will hardly find.

The red-skinned ones
do not wish me well –
they are eating flesh
and other foods they grow
below the dirt.

They stone me when I pass
and seize my iguana.

Silver like the moon
I see you, sprouting feathers
From your iron head.
You may fly into any valley
Like a loud parrot
and always twist my neck,
Christopher Columbus.

INAMORATA

In my deep dark mud-lust and rebellion
The red earth I wear like the long coats
Of the Spanish Cabildo, resonating with
The approval of my own salty legislation.

I command this and that:
Hitherto and hereafter as I wish.

I have no pox,
No gait that leans with gout,
No torn toes,
Or dilemmas.

The earth smells of sex again without dissent:
My face into it and my mouth tastes yam;
Her breath is sweet potato.

I wear the red earth by staying low.
The men are scraping dirt and scrubbing –
They do not have the coat that Joseph wore.

They do not wear the earth.
When they die
The earth will stitch their bodies
With her roots and vines,
Like stupid little buttons.

THE REGULATIONS

In the name of Lagahoo
The bushes are parted
And shrieks of children
Intermingle with broken glass,
And in nearby squares,
From atop their forgotten pedestals,
Throats made of stone and of brass
Blow mist thick enough
To tangle the ankles of mules,
Five miles away, grazing
In his most dark presence.

On a night like this a Governor will not sleep
But pace his halls with dreams of Orders-in-Council

CANE FIELD CROSSING

At the edge of a sea of cane I stood
then crawled through to the other side:
My nostrils were pistols smoking,
My knees were polished saucers,
My heart was shark skin boiling,
My mind was boll weevil, April, a gate,
My toes were fingers, fingers were smoke,
My skin was pumpkin's, swollen,
My nipples were oysters,
My eyes were carbide,
My back was sea-eggs,
My throat was glass,
My legs were goat's legs,
My vision was splintered, a quartz moon,
And I stood up on the other side, still breathing.

My time was three hours,

No. Four hours.

It was three hours it took.

THE CHANGELING

This is my sapodilla face –
Each eye a shiny dark seed,
Skin soft, brown, pierceable.

My sapodilla face is nearing.

This is my pineapple face.
Run your fingers gently,
It is not unshaven so much as thorny.

My pineapple face is nearing.

These are my Lagahoo hands –
Pressed behind your buttocks
Like a government railing.

My Lagahoo hands are unchanging

You may climb into any face.
The clouds climb into sky:
The sky is blue or the sky is grey.

Let your fingers dip
Into the brown pond of my eye
And spread a ripple to my outer flanks.

When I hear your calling
I will come with thanks
As flesh entirely of your making.

WHEREVER YOU BE

Come meet me by the sea wall
where the waves weave their foamy laces
and I will open your hands and your eyes
to the pearly moon.

I who am naked
on the rocks that breathe like stallions
will seal each crevice
of our vernal embrace.
Come soon to me
and wash my skin
muddied in a pit of remembrance:
I who took refuge
from your temples and cinemas,
the gravel that you pelted
the nails your hammers pounded.

I have time enough
to hold back evening
to curl it once around your ankles
like a dream

My head is stuffed with green leaves
and I am waiting for you
at the sea wall
with kisses contagious as disease.

TAMING THE WILD HOG

In the taming of the wild hog,
what I know of the small hog
I put to use against the large hog.

So too a noisy hurricane
accumulates its thunder
in a tin pail of morning drizzle.

The small things of the round land
explain the larger things:
the mountain begins from rocks and sand.

From this small page Lagahoo rules the world!

BY STONY PATHS

By stony paths
along the sea
where hibiscus blossom
the stony crabs
defy the waves
ceaselessly.

It is fierce
and unforgiving –
rocks like teeth
lean out,
the ocean
shoulders in.

Along the edges
of the surf
the swimmers
stare at me,
somewhere between
inconsequence
and enormity.

CHANTEUSE

Wishful thinking: a place

feet.   speed me quickly past there.
         the night encircles everything
         but I am running wild inside the day

anticipation: a fingernail of glass
smoke: the fist in the chest
Rome :   a book

mind.   lift me blindly past there.
         on my head soldiers' boots march past
         but they and I will soon be gone

religion: a field of gay flags
water: blood
desire: a mirror showing you   you
waiting :   16 birthdays, 15 birthdays, 14
                     and so on

eyes.   show me something not made of dust to
         fall before
hands.   unmake the gaping staircase going
         both ways.

Love: a contraption made with bone
idea: a noise creating words

mouth.   sing me further out to sea
         on a clear green day –
         far from tissues made of grease and lies.
         sing the whole life

veins flushed of turpentine
alabaster manes loosened in wind.
the empty holes inside.
the whole life sung
and me, too far out at sea
to care who listens.

DANCING

The Snake Lady rolls her buttocks past the tables.
                I am not an engine,
                        my milk is real.

The Snake Lady flings off an apron.
                        How can I love and
                                how can I love?

The Snake Lady's turn is next.

She enters from where darkness gathers in the room.

The night they are drowned in
                        rushes to her ankles,
Drains past their beards, stiff as coral,
Into the phosphorescence of her jeweled breasts.

The Snake Lady understands their dying,
                        why they sit there hooting,
                        sucking life out of stale rum bottles
                        and making threats.

THE WINDOW

O for love for love
I would be two suitors –
One to draw the blinds,
One to gaze upon you.

The night may be cold
Upon my shoulders
But I can linger
While dogs howl.

Dew mists the window panes,
Draws pearls across
Your sleeping face
and veils my wanting.

My eyes needed comfort:
and now they are enthralled.
For love I would stay forever,
Palms pressed against this wall.

LAGAHOO MEASURES THE WORLD

The furthest that my shadow travels
Is three days
To the ocean:
Then we separate as friends.

Shadows tentacle the land.

A man turns, shouting back
at mountains when they groan.
When I turn, the rain clouds crack.

I will not turn again.

The distance my arms encompass
is the whole webbed forest.
                  A thousand bounds separate
                  Mason Hall from Castara

The ocean's deepness   the wound's deepness
My blood gushes freely   out of holes

It takes ten days
of death

for the man's face
to fall off

but twenty years
of laughter

to make it
crease

ENTERTAINMENTS

Lagahoo throws a stone into ocean
and the water surrounds him.

Lagahoo picks up the scissors
and he is cut in two.

Lagahoo opens his eyes less often
because it is dark outside: eyes closed

and now a circus by de Chirico!

The closing of the book opens the mind
like the closing of the blood-shot eyes.

Numbers cannot count me or the stars
or the leaves that roll in on wind.

I can become words plentiful as sand
and still be nameless, even to me.

Lagahoo breathes in salty air
and sings you chords of cloud, drinks

ocean and spits anemone,
Portuguese Man O'War.

THE GARDEN OF EDEN

Your eyes were darting last night –
I was regarded
like a heartless hunter
stalking his nervous quarry.

What can I bring to you
but my own love?
It is carefully wrought
and smooth around the edges.

Last night it became
a howling
smothered by my hands
to the point of silence.

I am not wrong about you.
The things you believe of me
and the doubts you hold
cannot save you from your heart.

THESE THAT I AM

What is dangerous in me is the trunk of coconut
leaning landward in the gale –
        it might snap now
        no

        not yet, but damn! How
        great the danger if it does.

What is peaceful in me are the river pebbles
        gentle as cow's eyes
        flowing into chorus
        with the moss.

What is angry in me is not well known to me
        but it is like a thirst
        for cool water
        in dry season

        anger
        frees the poor
        more quickly
        than horses or paper –

        what is angry in me is thought.

The school boys playing in mud
and the mud
is what is alive in me.

What is dying in me are big roads in the forest
        with tractors on either side.

My long swim across the evening bay
                    are hands, reaching to hold the ocean,
                    one hand by one hand,
                    and that is what is deeply in me
                    and the other creatures.

EACH POEM I WRITE

Read me   Rope me
Roll into tiny balls
Ten round versions of me.

I feel betrayed by trees.
Chopped to chunks –
                         dead trees
Cannot prod me or prop me
or please me anymore.

I am pressed to the ground
by lies.
                 They have weight.
Lies have weight in their poisonous centres!

Wrap me tightly with scabrous wounds –
I am floating away too soon…
So wrap me instead with silent mouths
That open silently like wounds.

Joy waves its coloured flag
Past my window

Mocks me   mourns me   un-
Makes me   and is gone –

Don't dare say that this too will pass –
Each poem I write is almost the last.

MY PARADISAL BIRD AND ME

After the present hunger
Drove me out of joy

I found myself exhalted
In the company of the bird.

Imagination fed, I descended.
Sing, I begged, a song like this,

And make my body tremble.
The song I heard was new to me.

Shall I dance for you, I asked,
Shall I, too, whistle gladly?

Should I play the tambourine,
Would you prefer to sleep?

I am standing dumb in waiting,
My paradisal bird and me.

How sweet, how sweet
was this taking –

But how shall we each relate
And make a keeping

If our sentences
Do not meet?

EXTRACT FROM HIS DIARY

Last night old Mister Green
invited me to dinner at his house
and in the middle of the meal
his niece and his wife
shooed us quiet, saying:
"You didn't hear
a sound by the door?
Someone fiddling with
the lock, you hear?"

It was then, after some silence,
that his five grandchildren
all took to their plates together,
not being much concerned with villains.

I would have remained quiet
but it's funny to admit
and so I did
bringing much laughter to each face:
Do not trust your ear for villains
while eating blue crabs.

WIND, WATER, FIRE, MEN

Lagahoo takes his shape from the wind;
Wind has no shape, but
Gives shape to the sails of the men's boats
        and the shape of ocean hedges.
Without the shape of things to press against,
        wind has no shape,
And yet Lagahoo presses against all things
And all things against him,
And each and each are different.

Lagahoo takes his shape from the fire;
Fire has no shape
Except the shape of those it makes its servants.
Without servants, fire cannot be,
        yet Lagahoo has no master.

The shape of water is not caused by water,
But by the palms of Lagahoo's hands and his beaches.
Water tumbles through the ages
Much as it tumbles through the rocks,
Without hindrance.
Without Lagahoo, water has no shape,
But Lagahoo takes his shape from the water.

The shape of the man is the shape of darkness
But the man's senses are full of light,
And Lagahoo takes his shape also from the men
And their senses.

The day does not see the night,
Nor the sun the moon.
The word does not become the idea
Nor do the birds join the conversation of whales.

And yet in the senses of men,
The day sees the night
The sun sees the moon
The word embraces the idea:

And so Lagahoo came to touch his nature,
And know its shape.

SEDUCTION

As I break through underbrush
just busy about and about
I glimpse the sharp glaze of cobalt
so pure so fresh and bright
and the little bay with its ribbon of sand
is proffered to me as a present,
proffered, I say, because my body
like a hand, hovers above it
hungry for discovery or wetness or joy

and I can see the child-men who plunge
not being about and about,
who give themselves to its tugging
like Eve, the innocent, before her fruit
of discovery and wetness and joy

and my legs rub together
toes burrowed deep in sand
and I am brought reckless into water,
driven forward by the grief of turning back.

NOW AND AT THE HOUR

My Jesus
I am wilting,
My many mouths are feeding,
My muddy toes that tremble
Tell me nothing
Of the ground beneath their trembling

O my Jesus
Stacks of paper pass through me
And each contains a page of doubt.

The ox I was
Leaned against the big waves,
                    immovable –
I sliced them open with hooves.

Arms encircled me like ribbons
Of smoke or incense. I turned,
But turned only to the moon
And did not fall apart.

O Jesus here is the idol that was broken.
Hold the snake that was beaten,
Flung like the drunken sailor, overboard.

Here is the dagger of Isis
Here is the wonderful talking eye of onyx
Here is the bleeding arm hoisting the torn flag of a nation
Here is the world without end or beginning.

I come to the village of Carenage
To be bathed in blessings

But am entombed in waves –
I cannot forgive or be forgiven.

The Baptist's hands are on my head.
His pen wrote red words on my chest
That I am not meant to read.

My Jesus,
My art is dark
But its marrow is made of coral and crabmeat.
It rejoices now and then in boldness
But is blown in all directions like
The cane arrows, quaquaversal.

Re-made, re-born
My evaginated body is tossed against the wall;
I pass in and out and on
Turning around corners without turning at all,

Surrendering less and less
Because I have less and less to offer,
Because so much already has been lost.

LAGAHOO TAKES THE BUS

He whispers in his crowded berth:

"Your feet are bound and laced in leather,
Your women's breasts are held with wires."

Inside the cabin, his fingers twist
A handkerchief, and he perspires.

WORLD WITHOUT END

O footprint of blood at the edge of the green forest
O medicine of mud and dead leaves
O shadow of the ocean's manta-ray
O will of chalk, muscle of Mora
O orchid root that binds the mind's trajectory
O choice of equal paths
      of equal sighs
      borne past the thick jugulars
O destroyer of light, destroyer of shape
O storm
O terror of eyes and the eye's claws
O mouth forever gaping, forever sliced
O phallus, O wind of angels and bonfires
O final song of lust
O lust, more dead than dead eyes
O face of death powdered with green moss
O hideous shape made more hideous in the night
O violence of sun and jagged stone
O violence of thorns and insect mandibles
O comb of rain, black hairy cloud
O breast pierced by iron, pierced by broken glass
O tongue of cloud alive in the mouth
      O tongue that will not give in

O cobweb made of wrists
O wrists more brittle than the will
O dark shape
O guilt that crawls on its belly
O guilt whose saliva seals the fist shut
O guilt that wraps each poison berry
O terror of night, and the soul's marrow
O dark life
Always and ever O prison of bone.

MY BARE FEET ARE THE NEW GOVERNMENT

On mornings each toe throbs
in gentle comfort
under the blanket
but soon soon enough
I shove them into leather shoes
and stand and look out the window
and my feet seem pressed into service
or bondage, perplexed,
which they are
which they are.

Taking shoes off
is much like
pulling down statues
of dead dictators.
My bare feet are the new government!

DELIVERANCE

A gaoler walks within her house
A gaoler known to none but me;
Her husband sleeps so peacefully
Between the sheets and muffled shouts.

Through the fissure of a dream I sent him,
Into the cradle of the arms of the dead;
It was she who called me to their bed,
Her bare limbs wet and glistening.

And I would three times raise her up,
Into the mist of her furthest dream;
Yet no swoon will suffice or redeem
Or free her from the place she's locked.

THE FIRETAILS IN THE BUSH

The Firetails are whistling madly in the bush
A quarrel or rejoicing I know not which;
They could tear their throats competing with
This morning's lifting of another sun.

The smoky hills are prophets of the morning,
The scent of honey vine circling at her feet.

She lifts the Eastern veils one by one;
The growlers and sharp-toothed run
And the tongueless high note singers
from nowhere come to claim the light.

I cannot say which or which could end
And morning still endure;

But I keep my silences,
Quietly embracing
What silence has procured.

ANOTHER MEETING

I saw you illuminated tonight
Under the edgeless glow of the moon.

A few years back, and younger,
I remember spying you in public.

Someone hissed, "Have mercy",
And I, guilty for my years,

Had to turn my head away.
I'm older tonight

By the same years, but you,
You have bloomed

And made me innocent
Of the early admonition.

There was something then
That pleased my mind –

Kept secret all these years
Because my imaginings

Were advantageous and wild.
At the edge of childhood

You were poised –
Edge of innocence, edge of wistful sigh.

There is a music that is strangely playing
Through the course of the flowing years

And in the darkness I know the lyric
My spirit lost on hoping now prepares.

THE OLD CITY HARBOUR

The unlit salt-water and metal omnibus:
an oxidized cluster of rust flowers
sprouting from the crevice
of a kerosene tin,
the ocean crocheted by thick fingers,
its surface iridescing above the sludge
in a somnolent ooze of colour
and the crippled legs of the broken jetty,
straining to detach itself from this life
adjoining our smoky breath
and weaved-of-virus shore.

A sign says Do Not Swim Here,
but I am seeing corbeaux
walking on the sea.

THE CASTAWAY

The moon is bright tonight.
                    No more can I say hello.
My waving hand is drowning,
                    and says goodbye.

I have willed flowers into blossom.
                    My cheek was wet with rain.
I did a pirouette for your pleasure.
                    There was no clapping, just silence.

These past few months
                    the sky was dark.
From your eye there escaped
                    not the slightest glimmer.

The moon tonight is mine.
                    A cotton shirt can alert
a fleet of warships.
                    I was never recognized.

TWO MASKS OF DEATH

I hold these two masks of death,
Two faces that I wear interchangeably.
The one that's made of human flesh
Soon will tear, for its eyes are fixed
On the dark hole six feet under;
The one that's made of stone
Is death, it has no life save
That which the mind imparts.

Writing poetry is necrophilia.
I love the sound of dead words
Bouncing themselves into a sort of life
That lasts these mere seconds.
A poem is the final kick of the dying mule
And I am the boot prodding this heave of life
That torment has produced.

My disintegration is high entertainment –
That is how it always is. The cloak falls away
To show, not my fall, but the world's.
What is true of the world is also true of me.
I see the ridge of a hill, and the tall trees bending leeward
And I know that that too,
Together with a stench of rot, is where Nietzsche
And Plath lie in their glory.

Inside my chest is a cavern
With these words scrawled in dark silence.
My scream will not be heard by the vendor of mementos
near its neon entrance.

OWNING THE WORLD

Lagahoo turns around
in a field of cane
and the wind bristles.

It is the time of harvest.

Lagahoo turns around
at a country junction
at the village fair
in town
in a bright place
in his living room

turning and turning and turning
and turning
till the wind bristles
till the world is his

HER EYES WERE LIKE BENT TWIGS

Her eyes were like bent twigs or lanterns in the forest.
"This way home, Mister," they said, and I still follow,
... But my home is miles away from here.

Her skin was freckled, not like watermelon,
But like those faded coral sequins on a dress
You see in magazines, atop a marble stair.

Her smile was a joy, a bowl of fruit.
It had the effect of water that with 2 leaps
I could jump into on any given day.

Her hair was perilous like the Maracas Road.
A man could easily get lost there
On a dark night, without a periscope.

Her teeth were capable of magnificent bites,
Her lips were the edges of orchid petals,
The sound her voice made was digital stereo.

And I am like a waterfall, a frantic flowing,
Or a bright scarf blown by wind
When the sky is dark and the moon, emerging.

THE EYEWITNESS

They were floating in on dry wind,
Reaching out with claws
To grasp the gunwale of the creaky boat.

Only now they had returned, the nine of them.

First thing that morning they had flapped out
From near Drowned Sailor's cave;
Straining out to sea over dark currents
And against the wind, they found the place
And circled there, pelting their bodies
Into the flat water from painful heights.

All morning they thudded bravely,
Dropping like coconuts in high wind.
I do not know what fish they found.

To see these nine now returned, like blown leaves,
And there, by the shore, the blue skinned men,
Smiling with their women! I saw them sit
As I see them at the cinema,
enjoying something artificial.

The birds should have shit on them.

The birds are not clouds or flowers.
Their bodies hurt, lungs soaked with water
All morning beating back their death by hunger.

ACCOUNTING AT DAYBREAK

What is to be won again?   Nothing
To be held and swallowed?   Nothing
To be hoped beyond the furthest hope?   Nothing

What is to become of me, what?

There is nothing to seize
Except peace and mango bark.
Nothing to be taken or thought,
or captured and let free.

What is there to be created?   Nothing
To be united with guava roots?   Nothing
To be believed beyond the clouds?   Nothing
To be sliced with the fist?   Nothing
To be cast aside in the dirt?   Nothing

At the edge of the river I sit in silence.
The grasses and the butterflies are dying.

What is there to hold but air?
But running water?

THE OCEAN

Always and ever the tall trees in blossom
                    each proud flower,
                    and the whole sea
                    the breath of me
                    filling the valley
                    and the sky
Always and ever

Always and ever the patient moon,
                    the nightwind circling
                    round the globe
                    and starlight
                    and frangipani
                    and the travelling tide
Always and ever

Always and ever the distant song
                    and the voices rising
                    to the furthest star
                    and the tradewinds
                    and human love
                    within the furthest heart

THE LIFTING OF THE DREAD

Here's to the lifting of the dread, to the ball of hair
Choking us without strangulation
That is spat out suddenly without explanation;

Here's to the unnoticeable things that –
once noticed –
unlock the doors that lead us back

that remind us that everything is temporary
including this day, this beautiful day,
this moment of lightness seeping through the heavy sky

O let us memorize this moment as a prayer is memorized.

THE WEIGHT OF THINGS

Fire removes the weight of things. A church
snatched by flame climbs into cloud
as proud as the house where women fuck.
I have seen half a city removed by fire
and walked afterwards among the men.
Some looked only at their feet,

but others bounced with cheerful strides.
The weight of the city removed by fire
also made them weightless.
I am trying to understand fire
and all its uses,

                    and why some men
regard their feet so carefully
and some revel in clouds.

PERFECT HOLIDAY DESTINATION

I remember the cadence of flickering lanterns
and the pink walls and the balustrades
fetching songs out of the breeze.
At dawn the sea is coughing up
its coconuts and foam;
the waves froth like milk on a stove.

By noon, the waiter's grin
becomes unstuck
and I can easily rest it
on a huckster's tray
for easy sale
or exchange.

The woman with a scarf wrapped
tightly round her head
whispers as she reads,
nursing the memory
of so many dull husbands,
Olympian as bulls.

I do not think she ever spoke with them.

Do not move suddenly,
It is a grey hour.
Everything is leaning or whispering
Nothing will drop or be destroyed.

A young couple sword-fight
with their straws;

she, with the scrape
that his stubble left
like a mark of love
or disease.

The steam escapes as I slice my lobster
and I think of a fresh wound,
or maybe an old wound
fleshed out and smoking.

A SUNDAY EVENING

I could maybe sing a song
in praise of roses
and write your name
in patterns on my arm:

Three roads down
they might hear me,
an echo from a cloud:
but now is not the month or day
to be delirious or loud.

I do not wish to turn your head
with sentences of beauty;
there is beauty enough in what I see,
which I have recognized, silently.

The world I know is full of tricks:
language, meaning, motives, acts.
Whirlwinds gather round each moment
and what is true, soon bends and snaps.

I do not need to paint a fancy picture.
Fancy pictures tell a thousand fancy lies.
I want this plain
so you can plainly see

what is happening to me:
deep inside the self I inhabit,
beneath its scars and histories of regret,
you have stormed the lonely prison
where I slept.

THE SKY AT BLANCHISSEUSE

Let me draw a circle. So.
In the centre is me,
outside is the world I know.

I begin with me
(not with me-as-myself)
as the writing goal,
because I know myself best
and through myself see the world.

I am the binoculars *and* the eyes.

A stampede of thoughts
cannot create a lasting idea:
you begin with one thought,
held in the head as surely as a child
is grasped with both hands.

Do not mistake me. There is beauty
too in a stampede, but the idea of the poem
encircles it before the first words are heard.

It begins like this: a gust of breeze.
The air rushes through the architecture of the head
past the washerwoman's linens,
producing shapes on each taut wire.

Where the air originates, I do not know:
my interest is in shapes.

It can blow even once and I am billowing,
gently billowing in expectation
(I have seen the same
in punters at the racetrack,

when the configuration
of an outcome first begins to shape)
and I never cease to be amazed.

Think of the sky above Blanchisseuse,
and you, waiting for a falling star
in the fullness of the whole night sky.

The wind blows throaty from the East,
droning in the background. The wind is immaterial.
It is the star that matters,
the sudden fissure of light,
unzipping the black dome
of the sky's cathedral.

You are waiting, but just now;
wait a moment longer.

Almost now.

In a Blanchisseuse night in April
The sky will open, eventually.

Nature is breathing, I am breathing,
The circle is starting to tag the sky —
Where the star falls from, I do not know,
my eye wills it out of the heavens.
It falls for me
through a crevice where the universe folds,
and not only for me as seducer of the stars
or me as the spark lighting that celestial fuse:

I am the meridian and the distant poles,
Surrendering to seduction while I seduce —

a writer in the act of writing, yet still
an unbelieving reader of what poetry is produced.

HERE IS BEYOND THEN AND NOW

If a surgeon with a bleak face
should lean over me, or a
pedestrian or my wife or brother,
to say to me, James, it is hopeless,
and I know that I am dying,
I want you from my cabinet
to retrieve this tattered writing.

Say to them that though the ink
that crawled across my page, like life,
will hereafter finish, I am writing
at this moment now with ardour
and the moment is not lost to them or me.

There is no trickery here or posing.
To me my life has meaning, though
to you I am unliving. How soon
would I discard this pen, if now,
at this very moment now, it failed me?
The sound out of silence it has wrung
from paper plays on, even here,
for you and them; so instruments
of passion are alive more widely
than a term of years can parenthesize –
they echo through the starkest
valleys, not as sighs that wend
slowly to stop, but howls of joy
that ricochet and cannot end.

If you bury me, you bury
everything that's left of flesh,
not everything I am or was,
and heavy though my casket be,
these hundredweights of moments
I have made, will carry me.

James Christopher Aboud was born in Trinidad. He is the author of *The Stone Rose* (Paria Press, 1986), a volume of poems. His poetry has been published in *The Trinidad and Tobago Review, The New Voices, The Caribbean Writer, Graham House Review, Agni* and in the anthology *Crossing Water, Contemporary Poetry of the English- Speaking Caribbean.* His poetry has also appeared in the Internet journal, *PoetryMagazine.com.* In 1994, he was awarded the James Rodway Prize for Poetry by Derek Walcott's Rat Island Foundation. He was called to the Bar of England and Wales in 1984 and practises law in Trinidad and Tobago where he lives with his wife and three daughters.

A small selection of poetry from PEEPAL TREE PRESS

Marion Bethel
Bougainvillea Ringplay
ISBN: 9781845230845

These poems are sensual in the most literal sense – the poems are about the senses, the smell of vanilla and sex, the sound of waves – radio, voices, sea; the taste of crab soup; the texture of hurricane wind, and the chaos of colours bombarding the eye. Bahamian poetry is being defined in the work of Marion Bethel.

Jacqueline Bishop
Snapshots from Istanbul
ISBN: 9781845231149

Framed by poems that explore the lives of the exiled Roman poet Ovid, and the journeying painter Gaugin, Bishop locates her own explorations of where home might be. This is tested in a sequence of sensuous poems about a doomed relationship in Istanbul, touching in its honesty and, though vivid in its portrayal of otherness, highly aware that the poems' true subject is the uprooted self.

Frances Marie Coke
Intersections
ISBN: 9781845230845

Francis Coke writes with eloquent empathy and profound insight about the difficult truths of family relations, abandonment, loneliness, and the challenges of faith when hope is hard to find. She writes about Jamaica's poverty, violence, class divides and racial complexities with the same tenderness that she writes about its people.

Kwame Dawes
Hope's Hospice
with images by Joshua Cogan
ISBN: 9781845230784

Powerfully illustrated by Joshua Cogan's photographs, Kwame Dawes's poems make it impossible to see HIV/AIDS as something that only happens to other people. Here, AIDS becomes the channel for dramas that are both universal and unique, voices that are archetypal and highly individual – dramas of despair and stoicism, deception and self-honesty, misery and joy in life.

Millicent A.A. Graham
The Damp in Things
ISBN: 9781845230838

In *The Damp in Things*, we are invited into the unique imagination of Millicent Graham: she offers us a way to see her distinctly contemporary and urban Jamaica through the slant eye of a surrealist, one willing to see the absurdities and contradictions inherent in its society. These are poems about family, love, spirituality, fear, and above all desire, where the dampness of things is as much about the humid sensuality of this woman's island as it is about her constant belief in fecundity, fertility and the unruliness of the imagination.

Esther Phillips
The Stone Gatherer
ISBN: 9781845230852

Tracing a woman-centred movement from childhood to the contemplative maturity of elder and prophet, Esther Phillips's affecting new collection is the work of a poet of wit, intelligence, and maturity of vision. She uses poetry to test the meaning of experience, and to seek and find its grace notes. Located in the moving, breathing landscape of Barbados, and displaying a lyrical West Indian English, this collection marks her as a major poetic voice.

Jennifer Rahim
Approaching Sabbaths
ISBN: 9781845231156

There is a near perfect balance between the disciplined craft of the poems, and their capacity to deal with the most traumatic of experiences in a cool, reflective way. Equally, she has the capacity to make of the ordinary something special and memorable. The threat and reality of fragmentation – of psyches, of lives, of a nation – is ever present, but the shape and order of the poems provide a saving frame of wholeness.

Tanya Shirley
She Who Sleeps with Bones
ISBN: 9781845230876

'In the deftly searching poems of *She Who Sleeps With Bones*, Tanya Shirley considers how memory revolts from oblivion, what it can mean to be "haunted by the fruit" of desire – sexual, political, the desire for an "uncomplicated legacy," for home when home exists only as a memory we cannot trust entirely, a space we fear even as we continue to go back there. These poems startle, stir, provoke equally with their intelligence and their music. A wonderful debut.'
— Elizabeth Nunez, author of *Prospero's Daughter*

All Peepal Tree titles are available from the website
www.peepaltreepress.com
with a money back guarantee, secure credit card ordering
and fast delivery throughout the world at cost or less.

Peepal Tree Press is celebrated as the home of challenging and inspiring literature from the Caribbean and Black Britain. Subscribe to our mailing list for news of new books and events.
Contact us at:
Peepal Tree Press, 17 King's Avenue, Leeds LS6 1QS, UK
Tel: +44 (0) 113 2451703 E-mail: contact@peepaltreepress.com